The Transcontinental Railroad

America at Its Best?

The Transcontinental Railroad

America at Its Best?

★ ★ ★

BY ROBERT YOUNG

DILLON PRESS
Parsippany, New Jersey

For two dreamers:
Theodore Dehone Judah
and
Delone Bradford-Glover

Acknowledgments

I am indebted to Randy Kane, Robert Chugg, and Rick Wilson of the Golden Spike Historic Site for their important contributions, to the staff of the Eugene Public Library for their competent help, to Elizabeth Yonkers of the Rochester Historical Society for her assistance, to Debbie Biber for her editorial and interpersonal expertise, and to my family for their love and support.

Photo Credits

Cover: *t.l.* Library of Congress; *t.r., b.l.* The Andrew J. Russell Collection/The Oakland Museum of California; *b.r.* Utah State Historical Society.

Archive Photos: 32. Courtesy, Buffalo Bill Historical Center, Cody, WY: 36. UPI/Corbis-Bettmann: 57. de Grummond Children's Literature Research Collection, University of Southern Mississippi: 40. Library of Congress: 13, 16, 17, 44, 46, 60, 66, 68. The Oakland Museum of California: 30; The Andrew J. Russell Collection: 6, 8, 10, 19, 23, 26, 28. Southern Pacific Lines: 42, 47, 62. Stanford University Museum of Art AAA, gift of David Hewes: 12. Union Pacific Museum Collection: 24, 34. Utah State Historical Society: 2, 50. Map, Heather Saunders: 6.

Library of Congress Cataloging-in-Publication Data

Young, Robert, 1951–
    The transcontinental railroad: America at its best?/by Robert Young.— 1st ed.
      p. cm.—(Both sides)
    Includes bibliographical references and index.
    ISBN 0-87518-611-4 (LSB).—ISBN 0-382-39172-1 (pbk.)
    1. Pacific railroads—Juvenile literature. [1. Pacific railroads. 2. Railroads—History.] I. Title. II. Series: Both sides (Dillon Press)
TF25.P23Y68   1996
385'.0973—dc20   95-34910

Summary: Examines the building of the transcontinental railroad and discusses whether it showed the United States at its best or was an example of unfairness, racism, and greed.

 Published by Dillon Press
A Division of Simon & Schuster
299 Jefferson Road, Parsippany, NJ 07054

First edition
Printed in the United States of America
10 9 8 7 6 5 4 3 2 1

★ ★ ★   Contents   ★ ★ ★

ROUTE OF THE
TRANSCONTINENTAL
RAILROAD

Promontory, Utah Territory

ONE

May 10, 1869

It was a cool, clear morning in the desert of the Utah Territory. Thin coats of ice covered the puddles that had been left by the rain of the day before. A brisk breeze shook the sagebrush that covered this flat valley and blew at the American flag that had been raised on a telegraph pole.

The date was Monday, May 10, 1869, a day that would become one of the most celebrated days in the history of the United States. It was on this day that the tracks of the Central Pacific Railroad and the Union Pacific Railroad were to meet at a place called Promontory, a small community of tents that had been erected overnight. It was the day that the world's first transcontinental railroad, the railroad to connect East and West, would be officially completed.

Originally, the completion of the railroad had been scheduled for May 8. Leland Stanford, governor of California and president of the Central

Pacific, was to arrive by train at Promontory from the West. His train would carry other Central Pacific officials as well as West-Coast dignitaries, newspaper reporters, and some special materials for the ceremony. Thomas C. Durant, vice president and general manager of the Union Pacific, would be arriving from the East, also in a train filled with guests.

But Durant's train was delayed at Devil's Gate Bridge, about 65 miles southeast of Promontory. Heavy rains and melt-off from mountain snow had swollen the Weber River and weakened the rail-

The bridge at Devil's Gate

road bridge that crossed it. Durant and his party waited for hours as 200 men worked to strengthen the bridge supports. Still the engineer refused to take the engine over the bridge, believing the heavy engine would cause the bridge to collapse and the train to plunge into the river 50 feet below. For safety reasons the cars were unhitched, and the engine gave each one a gentle push across the shaky bridge over the raging river. Another engine, No. 119, was sent from Ogden to pull the cars the rest of the way to Promontory.

Excitement was in the early morning air at Promontory on May 10. Spectators lined the tracks as workers laid the last ties and rails and drove all but the last few spikes to hold them in place. The final tie to be laid by the workers was brought by Stanford from California and was made of polished laurelwood. A silver plaque identified the tie as

Although Stanford's train got to Promontory in time for the ceremony, it too, had some problems getting there. While crossing California's eastern mountain range, the Sierra Nevada, the train came upon a log that had fallen across the tracks. The engineer of the train braked hard but could not stop before hitting the log. A man who was riding on the cowcatcher, or frame on the front of the engine, jumped for his life and was injured. All the passengers were shaken but safe. The cowcatcher was smashed, and steps along the side of the engine were ripped off. The damaged engine slowly pulled the train to the next station. There it was replaced by another engine, Jupiter.

★ ★ ★ ★ ★

Workers from the two railroad companies took turns laying the last few rails. Irish workers from the Union Pacific laid the next-to-last rail. Chinese workers from the Central Pacific laid the last rail and drove a few spikes to hold it in place. When someone shouted to a photographer, "Take a shot!" the Chinese—knowing only one meaning for the words—dove for cover.

"The last tie laid on the completion of the Pacific Railroad, May, 1869." Four holes had been drilled in the tie to accept the special spikes that would be used.

About 10 A.M., Durant's Union Pacific train arrived at Promontory, joining the Central Pacific train. Officials from both companies shook hands and began planning the Golden Spike Ceremony that was supposed to begin at noon. But planning the ceremony was not easy. The officials could not agree on who would hammer the last spike. Should it be someone from the Central Pacific, since that company

Laying the last rail

10

had brought the special spikes for the ceremony and had begun construction first? Or should it be someone from the Union Pacific, since that company had built its line over the longest distance?

With only a few minutes remaining before the ceremony was to begin, the details were finally worked out. Representatives from both companies would get a chance to drive the last spike.

The ceremony began with a prayer, followed by the presentation of the special spikes. Dr. H. W. Harkness, a Sacramento newspaper publisher, presented Governor Stanford with two gold spikes, which Stanford placed into the predrilled holes in the laurelwood tie. F. A. Tritle, Nevada's railroad commissioner and a candidate for governor, presented Durant with a silver spike. And Governor Anson P. K. Safford, of Arizona, presented Durant with an iron spike plated with gold and silver. Durant added both spikes to the remaining holes in the laurelwood tie.

Speeches followed, first by Leland Stanford and then by Grenville Dodge, chief engineer of the Union Pacific. Dodge took the place of Durant, who was suffering from a painful headache.

After the speeches, Stanford was handed a maul, a heavy spike hammer. The maul had been silver-plated for this special occasion. Stanford and Durant took turns tapping in the precious-metal spikes. They tapped very gently so that no marks would be left on the spikes.

After the spikes were in place, the engineers of Jupiter and No. 119 took turns running their engines over the last rail. Then the precious-metal spikes and the laurelwood tie were quickly removed. Workers slid a regular pine tie under the rails and drove in three ordinary iron spikes. The fourth spike, along with the maul, was wired to a nearby telegraph. The entire nation would be able to hear as the final spike was driven to complete the railroad.

★★★★★★★★★★★★★★★★

Although there were two gold spikes at the ceremony, only one of them became known as *the* Golden Spike. This spike was the idea of David Hewes, a San Francisco contractor, who was upset to learn that no special spikes had been made for the ceremony. Hewes took some of his own gold, worth $400.00, and had it cast by San Francisco jewelers into a 5 5/8-inch spike that weighed 14.03 ounces. Two sides of the spike were engraved with the names of officials and the board of directors of the Central Pacific. Another side read "May God continue the unity of our Country as the Railroad unites the two great Oceans of the world." On the last side was engraved "The Pacific Railroad ground broken Jany 8th 1863 and completed May 8th 1869." Engraved on the top of the spike was "The Last Spike."

The Golden Spike

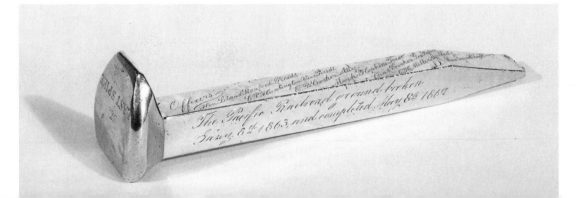

Officials shake hands to celebrate the completion of the railroad at Promontory.

Leland Stanford stepped forward and took a mighty swing at the spike. When he missed the spike and hit only the tie, the railroad workers who were watching roared with laughter. Next came Durant, who swung and missed both the spike *and* the tie!

Finally, a railroad worker drove the last spike into the tie. It was 12:47 P.M. when the Western Union telegraph operator—in the first nationwide telegraph hookup in history—sent the message the nation was waiting for: "D-O-N-E."

While photographs of this historic event were being taken in Promontory, the rest of the nation began celebrating. In Washington, D.C., a magnetic ball on top of the Capitol was dropped to signal the beginning of the public celebration. In Buffalo, thousands of people poured into the streets to sing "The Star-Spangled Banner." In New York City, soldiers fired a 100-gun salute, and Wall Street closed for the day. In Chicago, people jammed the streets in a parade that was seven miles long. In Sacramento, 30 locomotives blew their whistles and rang their bells as thousands cheered. In San Francisco, cannons boomed far into the night. It was a national celebration larger than any since General Robert E. Lee's surrender, ending the Civil War.

The first transcontinental railroad was the largest, most ambitious project ever attempted up to that date in our nation's history. But was this project really an example of America at its best, as we are so often told? Or was the transcontinental railroad a symbol of unfairness, racism, and greed, as some people believe? This book will present both sides and encourage you to decide for yourself.

TWO

A National Dream

The dream of linking East and West in the United States began early in the nineteenth century. In 1832, two years after the first steam locomotive made its trial run in America, a Michigan newspaper suggested that a railroad be built across the nation. In 1835, Dr. Hartwell Carver of Rochester, New York, made a similar suggestion and even asked Congress for a charter. The idea sounded crazy to many people because only about 100 miles of track had been laid at the time. Building a railroad across the country would require laying about 3,000 miles of track across deserts, mountains, rivers, and wilderness. Even if it was possible—many believed it wasn't— the costs would be staggering.

Despite the great challenges of building a transcontinental railroad, the idea fit in well with a popular belief of the time. This belief, known as Manifest Destiny, stated that the United States had the clear right to expand its borders; it was the

This painting by John Gast illustrates the idea of Manifest Destiny.

★ ★ ★ ★ ★ ★ ★ ★ ★ ★ ★ ★ ★ ★

In the 1840s thousands of Americans were heading west for gold, fertile farmland, and new lives. To get there, people had two choices—travel by ship or travel by wagon. Going by ship was long, expensive, and dangerous. The 16,000-mile journey took travelers around Cape Horn, at the southern tip of South America. Many ships were wrecked in the rough, stormy waters off the Cape. A shorter route took passengers by sea to Central America, where they next traveled overland through jungles. At the Pacific Ocean the trip continued by sea. This 5,450-mile route was often advertised as the fastest way (six weeks) to get to the West, but it was not cheap ($300) and was not without dangers. Many who traveled through the disease-infested jungles died of cholera, malaria, or yellow fever.

Traveling west by wagon train was not much easier. It was a long, hard journey filled with many dangers: attacks by Native Americans, bad weather, long stretches without water, and diseases. This trip took between three and six months.

destiny of the nation to own and govern all of North America.

People who promoted building a railroad across the United States used several arguments to support their position. One was that a transcontinental railroad would make it easier to trade with the countries of Asia. Goods could be sent by ship from China and Japan to the West Coast and then could be easily and quickly carried across the country by train. Another argument was that the railroad would be a better way for settlers to reach the West. Still another argument for building a transcontinental railroad was that it was needed to help settle the plains and protect settlers from Native Americans.

By the early 1850s there was agreement by many politicians in Washington, D.C., that a transcontinental railroad was needed. There was also

Clipper ships such as this one carried passengers around Cape Horn in the 1850's.

increasing agreement that such a railroad could be built. But there were disagreements, too. The most important disagreement was about which route the railroad would take across the country. The route was important because of the effect the railroad would have on the cities along the way. Such cities would have great economic advantages.

Politicians were very concerned about the route of the railroad. They wanted the cities of their own states to reap the advantages that the railroad would bring. Secretary of War Jefferson Davis, from Mississippi, wanted the railroad to take a southern route. Stephen Douglas, a senator from Illinois, wanted the route to begin in Chicago. Thomas Hart Benton, a senator from Missouri, wanted St. Louis to be the eastern terminal.

In March of 1853, Congress decided that it would need more information before it could decide which railroad route to help finance. The Department of War sent out five survey parties to gather information. Congress would use that information to decide which route was the most practical. Along with the survey teams went artists, botanists, cartographers, engineers, geologists, naturalists, and zoologists. Together they studied the land as it had never been studied before.

The findings from the surveys were disappointing. There was clearly no one best route, so the

Surveyors pass instruments up a steep cliff.

arguing continued and even worsened as hostilities grew between Northern and Southern states.

While politicians debated the best route for a transcontinental railroad, a few enterprising individuals were making surveys and plans of their own. Thomas Durant, then an executive of the Rock Island Railroad Line, in Illinois, had an idea for a transcontinental railroad. He hired a talented young engineer named Grenville M. Dodge to survey the land from Iowa to the Rocky Mountains.

Dodge spent nearly five years exploring and surveying the Platte River valley, looking for possible railroad routes. Dodge became an expert regarding this area, and he even sent presidential candidate Abraham Lincoln some of the information that he had collected. But then the Civil War started, and Dodge went east to join the Union Army.

The Civil War was a disaster for the United States in terms of lives and money lost, but the war was helpful in bringing about the transcontinental railroad. President Lincoln was concerned that the Confederacy—with sympathizers from the West— would attack the North from California. A railroad would make it possible to move troops quickly to the West and stop an attack.

Congress finally decided to support a transcontinental railroad because of the threat to the Union and because there was no longer any political objection to a northern route, since the states of the South had seceded. Congress passed the Pacific Railroad Act in 1862, and President Lincoln signed it into law on July 1.

The act authorized two companies to construct a railroad that would finally link East and West. The Central Pacific would build its portion east to the California-Nevada state line. The Union Pacific, with which Durant was now associated, would build west from the Missouri River, across Nebraska, over the Rocky Mountains in Wyoming, across Utah's Salt Lake Basin, and across Nevada to meet the Central Pacific line at the California border. Because of rivalries between towns that wanted to be the starting point for the Union Pacific along the Missouri River, Congress decided not to determine the starting point for the railroad. Congress left the decision to President Lincoln, who chose Omaha, in the Nebraska Territory.

The companies would receive 640 acres of land for each mile of track they laid. They could sell this land to raise money for construction. The railroad companies would also get financial help in the form of loans, which they were to pay back in 30 years at 6 percent annual interest. The companies could borrow $16,000 for each mile of track they laid on the plains, $32,000 for each mile of track they laid on the high desert of Nevada and Utah, and $48,000 for each mile of track they laid through mountains.

On December 2, 1863, the Union Pacific broke ground in Omaha. Since the nearest existing railroad was 100 miles to the east of Omaha, materials had to be delivered by wagon, then loaded onto riverboats to be taken through the dangerous currents of the Missouri River to Omaha, on the west bank. Some boats sank, and the valuable railroad materials were lost in the river. As a result, construction went very slowly for chief engineer Peter Dey and his crew.

Money was a continuing problem. In the spring of 1864, Thomas Durant, now of the Union Pacific, and Collis Huntington of the Central Pacific traveled to Washington, D.C. Their goal was to convince congressmen of their need for more help. The result of their efforts was the Pacific Railroad Act of 1864. This act doubled the amount of land the companies were given and made the loan money more quickly available.

Despite the increased support from the government, for the next year not much construction was completed by the Union Pacific. Dey had resigned, and since the railroad was still having money troubles, people were cautious about investing. Lincoln appealed to millionaire Congressman Oakes Ames of Massachusetts to assist. When Ames and his

Jack Casement of the Union Pacific Railroad is seen in the foreground of this photo.

brother invested more than $1 million, other investors followed.

It wasn't until midway through 1866, three years after the ground breaking, that the Union Pacific really began to make progress. With the Civil War over, thousands of men were available for work. Durant hired Jack Casement, an experienced rail layer and former army commander, to oversee the

★ ★ ★ ★ ★ ★ ★ ★ ★ ★ ★ ★ ★ ★

Jack Casement and his younger brother Dan were an important team to the Union Pacific Railroad. Jack was the field boss in charge of tracklaying. Dan handled the paperwork, making sure supplies were ordered and that the men were paid. Even though both men were physically small—Jack was five feet four inches tall and Dan was even shorter—they were respected for their toughness and hard work.

The Casements offered the workers incentives to get more work done. Each man received a pound of tobacco if a mile of track was laid in a day. If workers laid another half mile, they earned an extra dollar. If workers laid four miles of track, they were paid an extra two dollars.

tracklaying. On May 2, Durant hired a new chief engineer, Grenville Dodge, who had previously surveyed for him. Dodge, who had risen in rank to major general during the Civil War, organized workers in a military manner. In only six months, Dodge's crew of workers laid six times more track than had been laid during the previous three years!

The Union Pacific reaches the 100th Meridian.

By October 5, 1866, the Union Pacific had laid 247 miles of track and had reached the 100th meridian. Although the 100th meridian was only a line on a map, it had been chosen as the dividing line between the East and West. To celebrate reaching the center of the nation, Durant had planned a grand train trip to that spot in Nebraska. He invited President Andrew Johnson as well as other very important people of the day. The VIPs rode in brand-new passenger cars, ate gourmet meals, posed for photographs, and viewed entertainment on their three-day journey. Guests enjoyed a band concert, viewed vaudeville acts, and watched as Native Americans performed a war dance and then a mock battle. On the last night of the trip, Durant arranged to have the prairie set afire. From the safety of their cars, guests watched as 20 miles of dry grass burned, spectacularly lighting the night sky.

As the Union Pacific moved west, the workers had many problems to overcome. They had to get supplies even though they were hundreds of miles from a town. The Casement brothers solved this problem by developing a "work train," which followed the crews into the wilderness. The work train had about 12 cars and was pushed by 3 locomotives. The cars carried food, supplies, and tools. There was a sleeping car as well as a dining car. The work train was like a town on wheels.

Work trains like this one carried food, supplies, and tools. They also included a sleeping car and a dining car.

Getting railroad ties became another problem. There were plenty of trees along the route, but many of them were cottonwood, which was too soft to last long. Hardwood ties made of cedar and oak had to be shipped in at great expense.

There were weather problems, too. In the winter, snow and freezing temperatures made working difficult or impossible. The spring brought floods from the melting snow, and summer brought blistering heat and storms of raging wind and rain.

Perhaps the biggest problem for the Union Pacific was caused by the Native Americans. Tribes of Plains Indians were not pleased to see the coming of the "iron horse" to their territory. Groups attacked trains, tore down telegraph lines, and ripped up rails to try to stop the railroad. Union

One of the most serious attacks by Native Americans came on August 6, 1867. Near Plum Creek, Nebraska, a group of Cheyenne tore down telegraph wires and barricaded the track. When a telegraph crew came to repair the lines, the crew's train crashed into the barricade. Before the six men could get to their weapons, the Cheyenne had killed five of them. The sixth, a young Englishman named William Thompson, was scalped and left for dead.

The Cheyenne then pulled up a section of rails, added to their barricade, and waited for the next train. When it came, it smashed into the barricade and then off into a ditch. The men in the engine were killed, but three from the caboose escaped and warned another train that was close behind. While the Cheyenne ransacked the train, William Thompson crawled away carrying his bloody scalp. He survived, but his scalp was too badly damaged to be reattached to his head.

Pacific workers were given guns to protect themselves, and United States Army troops were assigned to protect the workers as well as the railroad.

There were more challenges ahead. The route through the Wasatch Mountains in Utah required the construction of four tunnels. And these came at a critical time; the Railroad Act had been changed, so now there was no fixed meeting spot for the railroads. Building the transcontinental railroad had become a race.

Despite the problems and challenges, the Union Pacific kept building. In 1867 the crews laid 245 miles of track. The next year they laid 425 miles of track, including a record-setting 7 3/4 miles in one day. By the time of the Golden Spike Ceremony, the Union Pacific had laid a total of 1,086 miles of

Dale Creek Bridge, the largest wooden bridge on the line

track and constructed the 650-foot Dale Creek Bridge, the largest wooden bridge on the line. The Union Pacific was slowed, but not stopped by anything—including rugged terrain, harsh weather, financial problems, and hostile Native Americans. In overcoming these problems, the Union Pacific became part of the greatest accomplishment of the nineteenth century.

THREE

The Real Costs of Building a Railroad

Building the eastern part of the transcontinental railroad was a great accomplishment, but its costs were great, too. Some people who have studied that time in history believe that the costs were too high. There was the great financial cost of building the railroad. But there was also the human cost—not only in lives lost but also in the way of life lost by Native Americans.

As the Union Pacific tracks pushed westward, towns sprang up along the way. The first was a place called North Platte, nearly 300 miles west of Omaha. During the winter of 1866, two thousand construction workers erected a tent city. It wasn't long before hundreds of buildings were constructed, including hotels, saloons, and warehouses. This town became the first of many communities that developed as the railroad extended west. These wild towns—Julesburg, Cheyenne, Corrine, Laramie—became known as "Hells on Wheels." When the railroad construction moved on, so did many of the people within the community. Some stayed, making them into permanent settlements.

People flocked to these towns to try to make quick money off the railroad workers. Saloon keepers, con artists, gamblers, and prostitutes provided countless opportunities for the workers to spend their hard-earned salaries of $35 a month. The result was wild and dangerous frontier towns.

At first Union Pacific officials did not seem to care how their workers chose to spend their money.

Corinne, Utah, a
"Hell on Wheels"

But when gunmen and other criminals began to take over the towns, Grenville Dodge ordered Jack Casement to do something about it. Casement did not waste any time organizing a group of ex-soldiers to change things. After Casement and his men shot and killed some of the tougher characters, order was restored.

These new towns were wild and dangerous places for everyone who spent time there. They were especially dangerous for the railroad workers; in fact, being in one of the towns was more dangerous than the work. For every Union Pacific worker who died in an accident on the job, four were murdered in one of these lawless towns.

In addition to the human lives lost during the building of the transcontinental railroad, money was lost, too—taxpayers' money. The Union Pacific received millions of dollars from the United States government.

But the money from the government did not come easily. Thomas Durant, along with Collis Huntington of the Central Pacific, worked hard to get the Pacific Railroad Act of 1864 passed. Durant spent thousands of dollars entertaining congressmen. He also gave them some stock in the Union Pacific in exchange for their votes.

In 1864, a year after the Union Pacific was formed, Durant and several other members of the

*Thomas Clark
Durant of the Union
Pacific*

board created a company to put out bids for supplies and construction and also to award the contracts. The men in this new company, which was named Credit Mobilier, could set the terms of the contracts at whatever they wanted.

The Credit Mobilier scheme was simple. The company bought supplies or construction services and then billed the Union Pacific at higher rates. For example, if a pick or shovel cost Credit Mobilier $1, they would bill the Union Pacific $2 or $3. If the cost for laying track was $30,000 a mile, Credit Mobilier would bill the railroad $50,000 a mile. The money that Credit Mobilier overcharged the Union Pacific was given to its stockholders as dividends.

Durant and other officials often received kickbacks as payments for construction contracts. When a contract was awarded, the contractor had to give a percentage—usually 10 percent—to Durant or other officials. Although this was unfair as well as illegal, it was the price of doing business with Credit Mobilier.

Credit Mobilier also made money by selling land that the Union Pacific had received from the government. This land, which bordered the railroad, had cost the Union Pacific nothing. Selling this land gave Credit Mobilier huge profits. It also

A major participant in creating Credit Mobilier was George Francis Train, an investor and publicity genius. Train was a friend of Durant's and was involved in promoting the Union Pacific from the beginning. He attended the groundbreaking ceremonies and then delivered what one local newspaper said was "the most tiptop speech ever delivered west of the Missouri."

Along with Durant, Train knew that more money could be made by constructing the railroad than by operating it. It was Train who located the charter of an existing financial agency in Pennsylvania, bought it, and then renamed it Credit Mobilier, after a successful French firm.

Train was a colorful character. Besides being in business, he was involved in many political and social movements of the day, including women's rights, communism, pacifism, and vegetarianism.

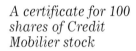

A certificate for 100 shares of Credit Mobilier stock

influenced the planning of where the railroad tracks would go. Sometimes the route would be planned so that the tracks would be laid over more valuable land. In that way, Credit Mobilier would get larger profits.

While the schemings of Credit Mobilier helped to make some people rich, it also made some people angry. Peter Dey was the chief engineer for the Union Pacific. He estimated the costs for the first 100 miles of track to be $30,000 a mile, but Durant wanted the estimate to be $50,000. Though suspicious, Dey agreed. But then Durant sent a "consulting engineer" to help make the route longer. It was clear to Dey that the longer route was simply a way to get more money from the government. Dey had

The Credit Mobilier investors made huge profits, but the Union Pacific workers suffered. By 1868 so much had been paid in dividends that the Union Pacific was nearly $6 million in debt. Workers who hadn't been paid became upset and angry. When Thomas Durant was on his way to the Golden Spike Ceremony, in 1869, his private car was surrounded by hundreds of railroad workers when it stopped in Piedmont, Wyoming. The angry workers uncoupled his car, pushed it onto a sidetrack, and chained its wheels to the rails. Then the workers demanded their overdue wages. Durant tried to get help from nearby army posts, but he was unable to get any messages to them. Finally, he sent a telegram to the Union Pacific office in New York and asked for money to pay the workers. When the money arrived and the workers were paid, Durant was allowed to leave.

had enough, and he resigned. "I do not care to have my name . . . connected with the railroad," he wrote in his letter of resignation.

Native Americans also paid dearly for the building of the transcontinental railroad. Although they did not pay with money, they paid with something much more valuable—their lives. Some lost their lives, but all of them lost their way of life. The life they had known was changed by the railroad forever.

At first, trains were mainly a curiosity to the Native Americans. In the summer of 1866, a Sioux chief named Spotted Tail took a party of braves and an interpreter to visit Jack Casement's construction crew, which was working about 150 miles west of Omaha. After the Sioux demonstrated their bow-and-arrow skills, railroad workers challenged them

When Native Americans of the plains first saw trains, many did not know what to make of them. One band of warriors tried to capture a train. They divided their group of 50 in half, then stretched rawhide ropes across the tracks and attached the ends of the ropes to their saddles. When the train came along at 25 miles an hour and hit the ropes, the warriors and ponies nearest the tracks were swung under the heavy wheels and killed.

to race their horses against the locomotive. As Spotted Tail stood on the locomotive cheering his riders, the engine slowly built up speed. Before long the powerful locomotive had left the riders far behind. The Sioux were in awe of this strange new vehicle that they called the Iron Horse.

Before long, the Native Americans' curiosity about the railroad gave way to anger. After all, the railroad was invading their hunting grounds. Their most important food source, buffalo, was being killed to feed railroad workers. And their living space was being sold to settlers.

This painting by Frederic Remington shows Native Americans hunting buffalo.

The United States government offered the Native Americans no help. The Indians were viewed as savages standing in the way of progress of the country's Manifest Destiny. As a result, the government ignored agreements it had made with the Indians. According to the government, they would have to accept progress and move out of the way. If they resisted, they would be forced to move or would be killed.

The Native Americans were not able to stop the invasion of their lands. The army and the railroad were working together. The army needed the railroad to move its troops quickly. The railroad needed the army to protect its workers as well as its property.

Despite the odds, the Native Americans were determined to fight on. In December 1866, the Sioux ambushed 82 soldiers near Fort Kearny in the Nebraska Terrritory and then attacked the fort with thousands of warriors. The next May Native Americans attacked settlers, stage lines, and telegraph lines. On May 25, a Sioux war party attacked railroad workers in Overton, Nebraska. All but one of the six workers were killed and scalped.

A hundred miles to the west, another war party attacked a camp of railroad workers while the camp was being visited by government officials. Grenville Dodge, accompanying the officials, tried to get some

For tribes of Plains Indians, the buffalo was more than the primary food source. It provided basic materials for shelter and clothing. It also served as a folk hero and religious symbol. The cultural and spiritual lives of the Plains Indians were based on the buffalo.

If the Cheyenne and Sioux had any doubts about whether they would be treated fairly by the government, they had only to consider what had happened to the Cherokee. In 1829 gold was discovered in northern Georgia, a land that had been legally deeded to the Cherokee. Thousands of prospectors swarmed to the area and demanded that the government cancel the deed. Nine years later President Andrew Jackson ordered the Cherokee off their land and used federal troops to escort them to a reservation in Oklahoma. That long, forced walk—during which many of the Cherokee died—became known as the Trail of Tears.

of the men to go after the Native Americans—but no one would join him. Angry, he told the officials that the government needed to eliminate the Indians or "give up building the Union Pacific Railroad. The government may take its choice."

The government did make its choice. Instead of working out a treaty that would respect the rights of Native Americans, or even living up to the ones it had already made, the government sent more troops to the West. By 1868 there were 5,000 soldiers stationed along the railroad between Omaha and the Salt Lake valley. Another 1,000 troops were posted at Fort D. A. Russell, near Cheyenne. The chance for Native Americans to save their hunting grounds and to save their way of life was gone forever.

FOUR

Building East

Like the Union Pacific, the Central Pacific Railroad began as a dream. In this case it was the dream of an intense young construction engineer from Connecticut. His name was Theodore Dehone Judah.

Judah knew a lot about railroads. He was a technical-school graduate and had surveyed several railroads in New England. His biggest accomplishment was designing and constructing a railroad along the Niagara Gorge.

In 1854, Judah traveled to California to build another railroad. This one was a 21-mile line between Sacramanto and the gold mines in the foothills of the Sierra Nevada. By the following year Judah's project was completed, but in his mind, he was not finished. He wanted to continue the railroad over the mountains and then across the continent. Like others, he too had a dream to build a transcontinental railroad.

Theodore Judah

Judah launched an energetic campaign to raise money to finance his dream. There were great advantages to having a transcontinental railroad, he told potential investors. It would help bring people to California. It would connect California with East Coast markets. Most importantly, a transcontinental railroad would save time and the great expense of shipping goods around South America.

Businessmen listened but were not convinced. They knew the truth about the Sierras: They were steep, rugged, and 150 miles wide. In the winter, heavy snows made them almost impossible to cross. So how could a railroad possibly be built across them?

Judah decided that he would need to provide people with more information before they would invest their money to finance his idea. To obtain that important information, he surveyed the mountains and searched for the best route for a railroad. Finally, with the help of Daniel "Doc" Strong, a pharmacist and an amateur surveyor, Judah found the ideal route. The railroad would pass the mining town of Dutch Flat, cross the summit of the Sierras by Donner Lake, and then follow the Truckee River into Nevada.

Judah was so confident of his route that he formed a company to build the railroad. He called the company the Central Pacific Railroad of California. After organizing his company, he searched for financial support. But it did not come easily. Many investors believed that building a railroad across the country was a huge gamble. Because of this cautious attitude, Judah changed the focus of his appeal.

Instead of asking for support for a transcontinental railroad, Judah proposed that a railroad be built into Nevada to take advantage of the recent discovery of silver there. A railroad would be a very practical way of getting California goods to the

Theodore Judah was tireless in his efforts to promote a transcontinental railroad. He organized a Pacific Railroad Convention in 1859 to try to get people interested. He traveled to Washington and tried to get government support. Judah told everyone he met about his dream of building a transcontinental railroad. He talked so much about his dream—which many people believed impossible—that he became known as "Crazy" Judah.

41

swelling population of the mining camps. Such a railroad would help California businesses expand.

Judah's plan worked. In June of 1861, he convinced seven Sacramento businessmen to invest in the railroad. The four major investors, who became known as the Big Four, were Charles Crocker, a dry-goods dealer; Mark Hopkins and Collis P. Huntington, partners in a hardware store; and Leland Stanford, a wholesale grocer.

The Big Four (clockwise, from top left): Leland Stanford, Collis P. Huntington, Mark Hopkins, and Charles Crocker

It wasn't long before Judah's excitement about building a transcontinental railroad spread to the Big Four. By the time the Pacific Railroad Act was passed in 1862, they were eagerly looking forward to being a part of this historic undertaking. During the groundbreaking ceremonies on January 8, 1863, Leland Stanford, who had become the governor of California in 1861, promised that the East and West would soon be connected by rails.

With barely enough money to cover the high cost of construction, the Central Pacific slowly began building east. When disagreements arose between Judah and the Big Four, they bought his interest in the company for $100,000. Judah was replaced as chief engineer by Samuel Montague.

Like the Union Pacific, the Central Pacific faced many challenges in building its railroad. But they were different challenges. The Central Pacific had a difficult time finding enough workers. Most workers in California could earn more than the two to three dollars a day that the railroad offered. People coming from the East had little interest in working on the railroad; they wanted to seek their fortunes mining gold and silver.

Charles Crocker believed that the answer to the labor problem was to hire Chinese workers. James Strobridge, the construction foreman for the Central Pacific, disagreed with Crocker. The Chinese were too small and weak to work on the railroad, he argued. Crocker convinced him, however, to hire some Chinese workers on a trial basis.

Strobridge was soon amazed at what good workers the Chinese were. They were tough and reliable and were willing to do any job they were asked to do. It wasn't long before Strobridge was calling the Chinese the "best workers in the world." The Central Pacific began trying to hire every able-bodied Chinese man in California. The Company also hired

Many Chinese laborers worked on the Central Pacific Railroad.

workers in China and had them brought to California. By 1866 there were 6,000 Chinese working for the Central Pacific. The following year that number rose to 15,000.

The terrain was another challenge faced by the Central Pacific Railroad. Thirty-four miles east of Sacramento, workers used black powder to blast a trench 800 feet long and 63 feet deep through a huge mound of dense rock. About 20 miles farther, they blasted a roadway into a ledge of shale that stood 2,000 feet above the American River. To set the charges for these blasts, Chinese workers were lowered over the cliff in baskets made of reeds. The workers drilled holes into the rock, filled the holes with powder, set the fuses and lighted them, and then were hauled up quickly before the powder exploded.

As the crews moved higher into the Sierras, the challenges increased with the elevation. Six tunnels had to be carved through the rugged mountains on the western side of the summit, and nine tunnels were needed on the eastern side. Crews worked on the tunnels day and night.

With its freezing temperatures and snow, winter slowed progress even further. In the winter of 1866–1867, 44 blizzards hit the Sierras. One storm lasted 13 days and left 10 feet of snow and drifts of up to 60 feet. Locomotives pushed a giant snowplow

*A Chinese laborer
in front of a
tunnel entrance
in the Sierras*

★ ★ ★ ★ ★ ★ ★ ★ ★ ★ ★ ★ ★ ★ ★ ★

Summit Tunnel was the most difficult tunnel for the workers of the Central Pacific to construct. It required a 20-foot hole through 1,659 feet of solid granite at an elevation of 7,032 feet above sea level.

Six thousand Chinese worked in shifts around the clock to carve out the tunnel. The workers stood shoulder to shoulder and used picks to chip away at the rock. They used hundreds of kegs of blasting powder every day. When workers could get a powerful but more dangerous, new explosive called nitroglycerin, they used that, too. Despite all the efforts, daily progress was measured in inches. It took about a year before the tunnel was finished. The Summit Tunnel is said to be the most expensive quarter mile in railroad history.

through the drifts to keep the tracks clear and take food and supplies to the workers. When the snow became so deep that 12 locomotives could not push the plow, supplies had to be dragged in on horse-drawn sledges.

Wind added to the winter problems in the Sierras. Raging winds pushed snow into giant drifts on steep ridges. When the drifts broke loose, avalanches carrying tons of snow tore through work sites and camps. Many workers were buried alive in the snow. Later, 37 miles of snowsheds were built to protect trains from drifts and avalanches.

Supplies proved to be yet another problem for the Central Pacific. Since there were few industries

A snow plow clears the Central Pacific tracks during the harsh winter of 1867.

in California, almost all the materials needed to build the railroad had to be carried from the East. Supplies were either shipped by way of Panama or around Cape Horn. Both routes were very costly in time as well as money.

In 1867, the Central Pacific decided to lay rails on the eastern side of the Sierras before the tunnels were completed. Supplies then had to be pulled over the mountain on sledges. A train was needed on the eastern side, too, so 3 locomotives and 40 railroad cars were completely taken apart, carried over the mountain, and then put back together.

By the spring of 1868, the Central Pacific had completed its railroad over the Sierras. That is when the race began between the Central Pacific and the Union Pacific. After the original Railroad

Building a railroad in the 1860s without the help of bulldozers, steam shovels, and jackhammers was no easy task. The transcontinental railroad was really handbuilt by skilled men with the help of animals and explosives. First the surveyors located the route. Next came the graders; they used plows, picks, shovels, and sometimes their bare hands to build a roadway for the rails. They cut through gorges, tunneled through mountains, and built bridges over ravines.

The next crew of workers placed wooden ties, or crossbeams, onto the finished roadway. Then ironmen dropped 500- to 700-pound rails onto the ties. These workers used notched wooden gauges, or "chairs," to space the rails exactly 4 feet 8 1/2 inches apart. Spikers followed, using sledgehammers to pound metal spikes into the ties to hold the rails in place.

Act was changed to allow the Central Pacific to build east of the California border, both railroads wanted to extend their lines as far as they could. And now that the Central Pacific was building on flat land, its work could move ahead more quickly. Daily progress soon was measured in miles instead of inches.

The land was flat, but it was hot. Despite the heat of the Nevada desert, workers averaged a mile of new track a day. Strobridge, the Central Pacific's chief engineer, made use of a work train similar to the one used by the Casement brothers of the Union Pacific. This helped him organize workers, tools, and supplies.

As the Central Pacific tracks moved east, it was uncertain where they would meet the tracks of the Union Pacific. As late as the spring of 1869, when the rails of the two companies were within 50 miles of each other, there was no agreed-upon meeting spot. Finally, President Grant got involved and encouraged the two companies to decide on a place to meet. On April 8, 1869, Grenville Dodge began a meeting with Collis Huntington in Washington, D.C. They decided that the rails would meet at Promontory Summit in the Utah Territory. Two days later Congress adopted a joint resolution supporting that agreement.

Later that month Central Pacific workers

demonstrated to the world how efficient they were. After Charles Crocker had boasted that his men could lay 10 miles of track in a day, legend has it that the Union Pacific's Thomas Durant bet him $10,000 that they couldn't. On April 28, 1,400 men from the Central Pacific worked furiously for 12 hours. When their shift ended, the men had laid 10 miles 56 feet of track, and they had won Crocker the bet.

A little more than a week later, the two railroad companies were ready to meet at Promontory Summit. They were *seven years* ahead of the original schedule. The Central Pacific had overcome many problems to get to Promontory. The company had overcome a critical labor shortage. It had overcome the difficulties in getting materials and supplies. It had overcome the harsh weather, rugged mountains, and the hot, dry desert. It had overcome all these challenges in building 690 miles of railroad. This was an amazing achievement!

On April 28, 1869, 1,400 Central Pacific workers laid 10 miles of track in one day.

FIVE

Racism, Greed, and Deceit

There is another side to the Central Pacific Railroad story. Most people acknowledge the great achievement of building the western part of the transcontinental railroad over mountains and through deserts. But there is a darker side. In completing its part of the railroad, the Central Pacific, like the Union Pacific, was guilty of racism, greed, and deceit.

The evidence of greed and deceit appears early in the development of the Central Pacific Railroad. Theodore Judah saw it soon after he returned to California from Washington, D.C., where he had helped get the Pacific Railroad Act passed. Charles Crocker quit the railroad's board of directors, appointed his brother to take his place, and started a construction company to begin building the railroad. This became an easy way for Crocker and his partners, the other members of the Big Four, to make large profits.

The Big Four wanted to build the first 40 miles of railroad as quickly as possible. In that way they could get money from the government. Judah disagreed with rushing the construction. He wanted the railroad built well and did not want to sacrifice quality for speed.

Building the railroad quickly was one way to get money from the government. Another way to get money was to convince the government that flatlands were really mountains! The Big Four argued that the Sierra Nevada actually began on the rising plain outside of Sacramento rather than in the foothills farther east. To support their claim, they sent the opinions of a professional geologist and two surveyors. When President Lincoln accepted their argument, the Central Pacific was able to receive contract loans of $48,000 a mile instead of $16,000 a mile.

Leland Stanford used his position as governor to help his company to build the railroad. He coaxed the California legislature to give the Central Pacific $10,000 for every mile of track it laid within the state. He convinced counties through which the railroad would be built to buy $500,000 worth of bonds. When the voters of San Francisco were about to decide whether to give the railroad $600,000, Stanford sent his brother to the polls with bags of Central Pacific gold to influence voters.

Rumors spread about the leaders of the Central Pacific. Some people believed that the Big Four had no intention of completing the railroad and that they were interested only in raising money to make themselves and their stockholders rich. Judah began wondering, too, and that added to his growing dissatisfaction about working with the Big Four.

Arguments between Judah and the Big Four increased. Judah did not like the way the Big Four did business. He was not satisfied with the quality of construction. He was unhappy about how the Big Four interfered with him in his job as chief engineer. Finally, he decided to leave the Central Pacific. The Big Four bought his interest in the railroad for about $100,000. In October 1863, Judah and his wife sailed for New York.

When the Big Four realized they could make more money by building the railroad past the California–Nevada border, they sent Collis Huntington to Washington. Along with Thomas Durant of the Union Pacific, Huntington used money to help influence Congress to pass a new Pacific Railroad Act. This act increased the amount of money in the form of loans and land that both railroad companies could receive from the government. It also permitted the Central Pacific to continue building east, beyond California, providing the company with the opportunity to get even more land from the government.

When Theodore Judah left California, he left with a plan. He would go to New York City, find investors, and then buy the Central Pacific from the Big Four. In that way, he could make sure the railroad would be built right.

While crossing the jungles of Panama, however, Judah caught yellow fever and became very sick. A week after he reached New York City, Judah died at the age of thirty-seven. His death came only seven days after the first rail of the Central Pacific Railroad had been laid.

The new Pacific Railroad Act greatly benefited the Union Pacific and the Central Pacific, but many people believed that it was unfair for the government to give so much support to private companies. Elihu B. Washburne, a congressman from Illinois, called the new act "the greatest legislative crime in history." Powerful businessman Cornelius Vanderbilt said, "Building a railroad from nowhere to nowhere at public expense is not a legitimate enterprise."

When people complained about how much money Crocker's construction company was making, the Big Four decided to create a new company to build the railroad. On October 28, 1867, they began the Contract and Finance Company. Its books were kept disorganized on purpose—to keep the finances secret.

With each mile of track earning more money for the Central Pacific, the pace of work picked up. During 1868, Crocker drove his men to the limit and completed 362 miles of track. Early in 1869, no point had yet been chosen for the Central Pacific and the Union Pacific to meet, so both companies continued grading as fast as they could. At one point, survey crews had overlapped nearly 200 miles, and grading crews from the opposing railroads were working so close to one another that fighting broke out between them. Finally, the government stepped in to help decide upon a meeting place.

Unlike the Union Pacific, the Central Pacific had little trouble dealing with the Native Americans. The reason is that the Big Four figured out a way to successfully work with them. Instead of *pushing* them off the land, the Central Pacific *bought* them off.

As a tradeoff for invading their lands, the Central Pacific offered jobs to Native Americans who wanted to work on the railroad. Tribal chiefs were given lifetime passes to ride in passenger cars of the Central Pacific's trains. Other Native Americans were permitted to ride free on freight cars whenever they chose.

The Chinese outnumbered all other groups that worked for the Central Pacific. But the fact that so many Chinese were hired does not mean the Big Four of the Central Pacific had an interest in providing opportunities for recent immigrants to the United States. The truth of the matter was that the Central Pacific was desperate for workers!

In 1864, things were not going well for the Central Pacific. Every payday nearly 100 more workers quit their jobs. They were tired of the backbreaking work and the low pay. Many workers were more interested in trying their luck in the gold and silver mines.

When Crocker advertised in California for 5,000

new workers, only about 800 responded. New workers were transported to the job site, but only two of every five showed up for work. Many quit as soon as they had earned enough money to get to the nearest mining camp. As the labor problem continued, Crocker became more desperate. He began hiring children, and he made plans for using Confederate prisoners. Then he came up with the idea of hiring Chinese workers.

Hiring the Chinese was a last resort because there was widespread prejudice against them. Californians saw the Chinese as being different. It wasn't only that people from China were physically small and had different facial features. They dressed differently, too, and they wore their hair in braids. They drank tea instead of water, and they ate rice, seaweed, and fish instead of beef, beans, and potatoes.

Because they seemed so different to many Californians, the Chinese were thought to be less than human. In the minds of many Californians, it was all right for Chinese to do simple jobs—to work as house servants or to rework abandoned mines. They could even operate laundries or restaurants. But people did not believe the Chinese had the skills or strength to be railroad workers.

It didn't take the Chinese long to prove what good workers they were. But despite their compe-

★ ★ ★ ★ ★

The long, braided ponytails worn by the Chinese men were called queues (kyooz). Queues were first worn in China after the empire was taken over by the Manchu tribe, in 1644. Manchu leaders made the Chinese men wear queues as a sign that they were inferior to their ruling masters. In California, the Chinese men wore queues so they could return home without being punished. Other railroad workers teased the Chinese for wearing queues; some even attacked the Chinese men, cut off their queues, and kept them as trophies.

tence, the Chinese workers were treated according to the prejudices of the day. Chinese laborers were paid less and were expected to work longer hours than other workers. They were the only workers not provided with bed and board. They set up their own tent camps and paid to have their food sent from San Francisco.

Working and living conditions for Chinese workers were very difficult. During the winter of 1866–1867, while the Summit Tunnel was being constructed, Chinese workers rarely saw the sky. They lived in shacks buried under snow. They walked to work in tunnels cut through the snow. Loud explosions and choking dust made their long work shifts hard to endure.

Leland Stanford, one of the most powerful men with the Central Pacific, became governor of California in 1861. In his inauguration speech he called the Chinese a "degraded race" and the "dregs of Asia." He also announced that he would support any laws that would keep more Chinese from coming to the United States.

A Chinese camp and work train in Nevada. Chinese workers were divided into smaller "gangs." Each gang had its own native cook and "head man," who handed out the pay and handled other affairs of his group.

When the hard work became really dangerous, the Chinese were chosen for the jobs. The reason was simple: Their lives were not as valued as those of other workers. So when men were needed to be lowered over the steep cliffs above the American River to set explosives, it was the Chinese who stood in the baskets. The foremen also knew of the Chinese workers' beliefs about explosives—that they scared away personal demons.

People working with the Chinese became more tolerant of them as time went on. They saw that the Chinese were hard-working and were often assigned the most dangerous jobs. Other workers also saw that the large number of Chinese workers provided the non-Chinese with opportunities for becoming foremen.

In the end, however, the Chinese, who made up nine tenths of the Central Pacific work force and who were an essential part of building the western portion of the transcontinental railroad, received little respect and even less recognition. On May 10, 1869, it was the Chinese workers who laid the last rail for the Central Pacific, but they did not have the opportunity to participate in the historic Golden Spike Ceremony. They were not even included in the photographs that were taken that day.

SIX

What Do You Think?

The Golden Spike Ceremony at Promontory on May 10, 1869, celebrated the completion of the first transcontinental railroad, but it was really more of a beginning. Because of the race between the Central Pacific and the Union Pacific, the work was rushed, and the quality of construction suffered. As a result, hundreds of miles of the railroad line had to be reconstructed. For the next several years, workers replaced bridges, enlarged tunnels, straightened sharp curves, and smoothed rough grades.

★ ★ ★ ★ ★ ★ ★ ★ ★ ★ ★ ★ ★ ★ ★

Isaac Morris, a government railroad examiner, believed that the transcontinental railroad was actually only two-thirds completed when the last rails were joined at Promontory. He pointed to many problems, including bridges that weren't safe, tunnels that were too narrow, roadbeds that were too narrow, and ties that were not spaced properly or that were made from wood which was too soft to last. In a report to Congress, Morris recommended that the government withhold payments of money and land until the reconstruction work was completed. His recommendations were not followed.

Despite the improvements needed to make the new railroad safe, trains began to run on the rails within five days of the ceremony. The trip from Omaha to Sacramento—a distance that took about six months to travel by wagon—took less than a week by rail. For a one-way ticket, passengers paid $40 to ride on wooden benches, $80 to ride in upholstered chairs, or $100 to ride in luxurious cars—with plush seats that could be changed into beds, steam heating, fancy furniture, and fresh linens daily.

A Central Pacific Railroad passenger train traveling through Nevada

During 1870, the first full year of rail service between Omaha and Sacramento, nearly 150,000 passengers rode Central Pacific and Union Pacific trains. By 1882, the number of passengers had soared to nearly 1 million per year.

One of the most important reasons for building the transcontinental railroad had been to make it easier for the United States to trade with China and Japan. Goods shipped to San Francisco could easily be carried by rail to the East Coast. However, within months of the completion of the transcontinental railroad, the Suez Canal was finished in the Middle East. This great achievement shortened the sea route from the Orient to the United States by several thousand miles. Goods could then be more cheaply shipped to North America's East Coast without using the railroad.

While the transcontinental railroad did not help improve trade with China and Japan, it did begin a new era of railroad building. During the 1880s alone, more than 40,000 miles of rail were laid in the West. By 1893, there were five transcontinental railroad lines spanning the nation.

As railroads crisscrossed the West, it was only a matter of time before more people began to settle the land. Encouraged by railroad-company ads, discount fares, and inexpensive land prices, thousands traveled west. More Western acres were settled

A Union and Central Pacific Railroad advertisement

between 1870 and 1900 than had been settled in the previous two and a half centuries! And by 1912 the last of the original 48 states had been admitted to the Union.

Many people found that Western life was not what they had hoped for or were led to believe. Blizzards, droughts, fires, floods, and grasshoppers drove some settlers back to the places from which they had come. High freight rates charged by the railroad companies often made it difficult to earn a living.

The transcontinental railroad helped to unite the nation as well as to populate the West. But this great achievement did not come about without its scandals. In 1872, after a public struggle for leadership of the Union Pacific between Congressman Oakes Ames, who also managed Credit Mobilier, and Union Pacific's Thomas Durant, Congress decided to investigate. The investigation revealed

Settling the West was not as easy as the railroad companies wanted people to believe. Some scientists, such as John Wesley Powell, warned people about the problems of settling the West. After studying land use in the Far West, Powell reported about droughts and the need for getting water to the dry land in order to farm it.

During his nearly 30 trips west, Powell also studied the Native Americans and made recommendations to the government. He suggested that Americans try to learn more about Native American cultures and make a real effort to treat them more humanely.

that of the $73 million the government had provided to the Union Pacific, only $50 million was the true cost. It also revealed that Ames had bribed other congressmen by making Credit Mobilier stock available to them for almost nothing. The stock was given so that congressmen would support issues of concern to the Union Pacific. As Ames put it, "I have found there is no difficulty in inducing men to look after their own property." After the investigation, Congress voted to censure Ames. He returned to Massachusetts a disgraced man. Soon afterward, he died of a stroke.

Next the attention of the nation turned to the Central Pacific. Congress wanted to know how the company had run its business in building the railroad. Fortunately for the company, its headquarters had recently burned, and all the records had been destroyed. Even so, Congress learned that the Big Four had made huge profits—$63 million—in building the Central Pacific. But no crimes were proven, and no one was charged.

Other people involved in the story of the transcontinental railroad were not as fortunate as the Big Four. Some of the thousands of Chinese laborers went south to work on other railroad lines. Most, however, moved to California and worked at factory jobs. By 1875, Chinese Americans made up 75 percent of San Francisco's woolen workers, 90 percent of the cigar makers, and a majority of its shoe and clothing makers.

Many people viewed the Chinese as threats to their jobs. As a result the Chinese were subjected to physical attacks, unfair laws, and discrimination. In San Francisco the Chinese were forced to live within an area only seven blocks by three blocks. Chinese workers were paid lower wages than whites received, and they were not allowed to join unions.

In an effort to improve their living and working conditions, Chinese Americans formed organizations. They challenged unfair laws and created protection patrols to prevent the growing number of physical attacks on their people. But their efforts failed to stop the hostilities against the Chinese.

In fact, hostilities against the Chinese worsened. In 1882, Congress passed the Chinese Exclusion Act, which prohibited Chinese from entering the United States for ten years. Only merchants, students, teachers, and visitors from China were allowed in, and those only temporarily. In 1892 and again in 1902, Congress extended the time limit. This law continued until 1943.

Another group of people who fared poorly as a result of the transcontinental railroad was the Native Americans, who used many parts of the West as their homes and hunting grounds. Many other Americans thought that the Native Americans were occupying valuable land that could be sold and developed and that they needed to be moved off the land. Some of the land was bought cheaply from the Native Americans. Most of it was just taken.

The buffalo, which was essential to the Plains Indians, became a target for white hunters. What started as a means to feed railroad workers became a national fad, in which it was fashionable to hunt

The railroad brought white hunters who slaughtered the buffalo.

buffalo from the windows of moving trains. Buffalo tongues were pickled and sent east to be served in the best restaurants. Hides were made into clothing, rugs, and footwear. Between 1865 and 1885, nearly 12 million buffalo were killed.

Native Americans resisted as best they could, but their weapons were no match for the firepower of the United States soldiers. Native American horses could not compete with the power of the iron horses. Even when the Native Americans won a battle—such as the Battle of the Little Bighorn, in which the Sioux defeated General George Armstrong Custer—the victory did little to help them win the war to protect their lands. In the end, the railroads helped to defeat all the tribes that resisted.

With time came changes to the railroad, too. In 1883, the Central Pacific Railroad was reorganized, and its name was changed to Southern Pacific Railroad. In 1904, the Lucin Cutoff, a shortcut across the Great Salt Lake, was opened to trains. Afterward, rail traffic through Promontory slowed and then eventually stopped in 1938. In 1942, during the Second World War, rails along the Promontory route were taken up so that the metal could be used in the war effort. Since then, a mile and a half of track has been replaced at Promontory and is part of the Golden Spike Historic Site.

What became of the laurelwood tie, the silver-plated maul, and the precious-metal spikes used in the Golden Spike Ceremony? The tie was sent back to California after the ceremony and was displayed in the Southern Pacific Railroad's San Francisco office. It was destroyed there in the earthquake and fire of 1906. The silver-plated maul was given to Leland Stanford and became part of the collection at Stanford University museum in Palo Alto, California. The engraved gold spike and the silver spike were also added to the museum. The spike that was presented by the Arizona Territory became part of the Smithsonian's transportation museum in Washington, D.C. No one knows what became of the second gold spike.

*Weber Canyon in Utah, one of the deep gorges through which
the transcontinental railroad passed*

Now that you've read about the first transcontinental railroad, what do you think? Was it really America at its best? The people who believe that it was support their view with the following points:

1. The railroad helped unite the country and settle the West.

2. It greatly improved transportation and communication.

3. The railroad companies overcame great hardships, including financial problems, labor shortages, difficult terrain and weather, and hostile Native Americans.

4. The railroad was completed much sooner than expected.

People who believe that building the first transcontinental railroad did not show America at its best use other points to support their view:

1. The railroad companies used money to influence voters and politicians, and they cheated the government out of millions.

2. The Central Pacific took advantage of Chinese laborers.

3. The Union Pacific permitted wild and dangerous towns to develop as its rail line moved west.

4. The railroad helped push Native Americans off lands that were rightfully theirs.

Which side is correct? Was this an example of America at its best? Or was it America at its worst? You have read about both sides of this issue. Now consider them carefully. What do you think?

★ ★ ★   Time Line   ★ ★ ★

1830   The first steam locomotive makes a trial run in America

1830s   Suggestions are made that a railroad be built across the nation

1840s   Gold is discovered in California; thousands of people rush for the riches

1853   Congress funds survey parties to gather information to help plan the route of a transcontinental railroad

1859   Theodore Judah organizes the Pacific Railroad Convention to interest people in building a transcontinental railroad

1860   Abraham Lincoln is elected President

1861   **April** The Civil War begins

        June Judah finds investors for his Central Pacific Railroad Company

1862   The Pacific Railroad Act is passed, authorizing the Union Pacific and the Central Pacific to build a railroad that would link East and West

1863   **January** The Central Pacific Railroad Company breaks ground in Sacramento

October Judah is bought out by the Big Four; he leaves for New York to find investors to help him regain control of the Central Pacific

November Judah dies from yellow fever

December The Union Pacific breaks ground in Omaha

1864   The Pacific Railroad Act of 1864 is passed

Credit Mobilier is organized by Thomas Durant and George Francis Train

1865   Abraham Lincoln is assassinated.

The Civil War ends, making more workers available to the Union Pacific

The Central Pacific begins hiring Chinese workers

1866 **October** The Union Pacific reaches the 100th meridian

Winter The first Hell on Wheels is constructed in North Platte, Nebraska Territory

1867 **Winter** Forty-four blizzards hit the Sierra Nevada, slowing construction

August Cheyenne Indians attack a Union Pacific train near Plum Creek, Nebraska

1868 **Spring** The Central Pacific completes its railroad over the Sierras

1869 **April 9** Officials of the railroad companies agree on a place for the rails to meet

April 28 Central Pacific workers lay 10 miles of track in a day

May 10 The Golden Spike Ceremony is held to celebrate the completion of the world's first transcontinental railroad

May 15 Transcontinental rail service begins

November 16 Suez Canal is completed, linking Gulf of Suez and Mediterranean Sea

1870s   Millions of buffalo are slaughtered on the Plains

1872   Congress investigates Credit Mobilier

1880s   More than 40,000 miles of track are laid in the West

1882   Congress passes the first Chinese Exclusion Act to prohibit Chinese from entering the United States for a period of 10 years

1883   The Central Pacific is reorganized and named the Southern Pacific Railroad

1893   Five transcontinental rail lines cross the United States

★ ★ ★   Glossary   ★ ★ ★

botanist—A scientist who studies plants

cartographer—A person who makes maps

censure—To officially criticize

cowcatcher—An iron frame at the front of a locomotive to clear the track; also known as a pilot

engineer—A person trained in the design, construction, and operation of structures, equipment, and systems

geologist—A scientist who studies the structure of the earth and its history

Hells on Wheels—Wild frontier towns that developed as the railroads were built

Manifest Destiny—The belief, held in the 1800s, that the United States was meant to extend its borders

maul—A heavy hammer used to drive spikes

meridian—A circle on a map passing through the North and South Poles; helps to measure distance

naturalist—A person who studies plants and animals in their natural environments

pacifism—Opposition to war or violence as a way of settling disputes

prejudice—The judging of a group of people on the basis of certain characteristics that all members of the group are thought to possess. Individual members of the group are not judged on their own characteristics.

queue—A long pigtail worn by a Chinese man

secede—To withdraw formally from an organization or political group, such as the United States

sledge—A sled on low runners, drawn by work horses, and used to move loads across snow and ice

transcontinental—Something that crosses a continent

zoologist—A scientist who studies animals

★ For Further Reading ★

If you would like to know more about the transcontinental railroad, here are some books that were helpful in writing *The Transcontinental Railroad: America at Its Best?*

Brown, Dee. *Hear that Lonesome Whistle Blow.* New York: Holt, Rinehart & Winston, 1977.

Combs, Barry. *Westward to Promontory.* New York: Crown, 1986.

Fisher, Leonard Everett. *Tracks Across America.* New York: Holiday House, 1992.

Jensen, Oliver. *The American Heritage History of Railroads in America.* New York: American Heritage, 1975.

Katz, William Loren. *The Civil War to the Last Frontier, 1850–1880s.* Austin, TX: Steck-Vaughn, 1993.

Kraus, Hans. *High Road to Promontory.* Palo Alto, CA: American West, 1969.

Mayer, Lynne Rhodes, and Kenneth E. Vose. *Making Tracks.* New York: Praeger, 1975.

O'Connor, Richard. *Iron Wheels and Broken Men.* New York: G.P. Putnam's Sons, 1973.

Wheeler, Keith. *The Railroaders.* New York: Time-Life, 1973.

For more information about the Golden Spike Ceremony, write Golden Spike National Historic Site, P.O. Box 897, Brigham City, Utah 84302.

★ ★ ★ ★ Index ★ ★ ★ ★

★ ★ About the Author ★ ★

Robert Young has been fascinated with the past ever since he walked through the house in which George Washington once lived. Besides writing books that help bring history alive, Robert job-shares a teaching position and visits schools to speak about writing. The author of 12 books for children and teachers, Robert lives in Eugene, Oregon, with his wife, Sara, and their son, Tyler.